Methods and Techniques of Teaching Basic English
—for the Teachers of Tomorrow—

児童英語教育のための方法と技術

青木雅幸（著）
Peter Williams（監修）

PREFACE

English teaching plays an important role in Japanese society these days, because the country has become more internationalized and welcomes more than twenty million tourists from abroad each year. It is expected to provide students with enough language education to meet the requirements arising from such fields as transportation, accommodation, catering, international trade and tourism.

The government of Japan, therefore, has started to underline the importance of English education, and has been expanding it to include younger children in elementary schools. To meet the educational guidelines set by the government, elementary school teachers are now required to teach English to students from the third grade, and probably even from the first grade in the near future. Following curriculum changes in the Japanese school system, teacher training has been required to catch up to the new trend in teaching English.

This textbook is designed for teacher trainees, who are preparing to teach basic-level English at elementary schools. It will enable them to learn (1) more English for their own personal use, (2) how to adopt the teaching methods proposed in this textbook, (3) basic-level English teaching methods and skills for their future careers, and (4) new trends in basic-level English teaching in this Internet age. It is absolutely necessary for teacher trainees to actually put into practice what they learn from this textbook, as theoretical knowledge alone does not make a good teacher, because teaching is a practical profession.

This textbook contains 16 chapters, each of which presents teacher trainees with an English teaching situation in an elementary school. Each chapter begins with a vocabulary preview and a keynote reading article that explains the target theme of the chapter, such as "Forming a Good Relationship with Students," "British English and American English," "Teaching Aids," or "Utilizing the Internet as Teaching Resources."

The Keynote Reading is followed by such activities as "Important Phrases/Words in the Keynote Reading," "Listening Activity," "Further Study," "Keeping a Class Journal," and "Discussion Topics." All of these are deeply linked to actual English teaching methods in elementary schools. Teacher trainees are, therefore, expected to learn the useful phrases and words from the keynote reading, and to practice the dialogue with their peers so that they will be able to make use of these expressions in practice when actually teaching students and children.

There are two main characters in this textbook; Keiko-sensei, a homeroom teacher (HRT), and David, an assistant language teacher (ALT). They appear in the dialogue section as well as in the class journal section of almost all chapters, so that you can compare yourself to the HRT and learn from the ALT. The character introductions including the other two ALTs are shown below.

By understanding the reading and dialogue sections and doing the accompanying activities, users of this textbook will be sure to gain confidence in teaching basic-level English.

Good luck, future colleagues.

The Author

Character Introductions

Homeroom Teacher (HRT)
Keiko

Keiko Watanabe is a Japanese teacher. She is a homeroom teacher of Class 5B. Her students call her Keiko-sensei. She does not speak good English, but she is very interested in studying and teaching English.

Assistant Language Teachers (ALTs)
David

David Smith is from Idaho, USA. He is a very popular ALT working together with Keiko-sensei, and helps her a lot. He is not a good speaker of Japanese, but he knows a lot about computer technology.

Kevin
Kevin is an ALT from London, UK.

Leonard
Leonard is an Italian-American ALT.

Contents

Introduction: Setting the Scene 6

Chapter **1**
Forming a Good Relationship with Students 10

Chapter **2**
Cooperation with Assistant Language Teachers 14

Chapter **3**
Groupism 18

Chapter **4**
Inter-lingual Interference 22

Chapter **5**
British English and American English 26

Chapter **6**
Teaching Aids 30

Chapter **7**
Using the Tablet Computer in Class 34

Chapter **8**
Utilizing the Internet as Teaching Resources 38

Chapter **9**
Untranslatable Expressions *42*

Chapter **10**
Slang and Informal English Expressions *46*

Chapter **11**
Practicing English with Other Activities *50*

Chapter **12**
Gestures—Non-verbal Communication *54*

Chapter **13**
Foreign Loan Words *58*

Chapter **14**
ESL vs. EFL *62*

Chapter **15**
An Additional Reason for Studying English *66*

Chapter **16**
Assessing English Ability *70*

Appendix: **Interview Test, Quick Reference for Classroom English**

Introduction: Setting the Scene

When the ALT Comes to Your School for the First Time

Below is a sample dialog between the assistant language teacher (ALT) and the head teacher (HT) supposing the ALT comes to your school for the first time. Listen to the recording and fill in the blanks and then answer the following questions.

ALT: Are you Ms. Tanaka, the Head Teacher?

HT: Yes, I am. Are you Mr. David Smith?

ALT: Yes, that's right. Nice to meet you, Ms. Tanaka.

HT: Very nice to meet you, David. Call me Junko.

ALT: I heard you have 1._____ about my duties at your school.

HT: That's right, but they are quite simple. Do you have a smart phone with you?

ALT: Yes, I do, but why?

HT: First, you can 2._____ and find important information about our daily schedule. It's written in both Japanese and English.

ALT: Oh, that's neat.

HT: Please check it every morning.

ALT: I will. What time should I 3._____?

HT: You should be here by 8:30. If you are late or absent for any reason, please call 4._____.

ALT: I understand, Junko. Do you have any dress code?

HT: Not really, but semi-formal or smart casual is quite okay.

ALT: I see. Do I have to wear a suit 5._____ like the graduation ceremony?

HT: Oh yes, a dark suit is recommended, David.

ALT: Where should I store my indoor shoes?

HT: Please keep them 6._____ with your name on it in the entrance hall.

ALT: I understand.

HT: You will have 7._____ with Ms. Keiko Watanabe, or Keiko-sensei. She will tell you about the day's lessons. I'll introduce you to her later.

ALT: Thank you. Could you tell me about the lesson periods?

HT: Each lesson is 8._____. The first class starts at 8:50 and ends at 9:35. There is a five-minute break between the first and second class, and a 15-minute break between the second and third class. After the fourth class we have a 40-minute lunch break and 9._____.

ALT: Wow, that's complicated. Do I have to return to the teachers' room during each break?

HT: No, 10._____, but students would be happy to talk to you in English during breaks.

ALT: When is the dismissal time for students?

HT: The sixth class finishes at 3:25 in the afternoon. Students have 11._____ _____ of about 20 minutes and usually leave before 4 p.m.

ALT: 12._____, what subjects do they study at school?

HT: They study such subjects as math, science, social studies, music, drawing and crafts, P.E., home economics, moral education, and Japanese.

ALT: 13._____ about Japanese people is totally true. Japanese students and teachers are really hard workers, aren't you?

HT: Yes, we are, David. I will show you 14._____ where you can keep your belongings and teaching materials. Follow me, please.

Questions

1. What should the ALT do in case he is late for school?
   _____

2. What time should the ALT arrive at school?
   _____

3. Where should the ALT keep his indoor shoes?
   _____

4. How long is one lesson period?
   _____

5. What do students do after a lunch break?
   _____

6. Does the ALT have to return to the teachers' room during each break?
   _____

7. What subjects do students study at school apart from English? Name five of them.
   _____

8. Where can the ALT keep his belongings and teaching materials?
   _____

Introducing Our School and School Life

Read the passage below written by Keiko-sensei and learn the vocabulary in bold type regarding school facilities, equipment, stationery, teaching aids and tools, and annual events. Then, fill in the spaces with at least seven examples of each category.

3

I would like to tell you about the school where I work because our **school building** is brand new and well equipped. The **principal's office**, **teachers' room**, and **nurse's office** are on the first floor. The **science room**, **art room**, **music room**, **library** and **audio-visual room** are on the second floor. Our **classrooms** are on the second and third floors. There are two **washrooms** on each floor; one is for boys and the other for girls. Next to the school building, there is a **swimming pool** and a **gym**, where we have **P.E.** classes. The **schoolyard** is large and equipped with three **swings**, two **slides**, one **jungle gym**, two **monkey bars**, a pair of **soccer goals** and a big **flowerbed** where there are flowers all the year round. The **school gate** is open when students enter and leave the **school grounds**.

There is a large **blackboard** on the front wall of the classroom. There is a large **world map** and a **class timetable** on the back wall. In front of the blackboard, there is a **teacher's desk** on which there is a **blackboard eraser** and some sticks of **colored chalk**. The **teacher's locker** is full of **teaching aids and tools** and **stationery**, such as **textbooks**, **notebooks**, a **pencil sharpener**, **pencils**, **erasers**, **mechanical pencils**, **ballpoint pens**, **markers**, **highlighter pens**, **colored pencils**, **crayons**, **drawing paper**, a **ruler**, a **set square**, a **protractor**, **compasses**, a **calculator**, **scissors**, **glue sticks**, **staplers**, a **Scotch tape dispenser**, and a lot of **print-outs**.

In the science room, there are many **scales**, **test tubes**, **microscopes**, **globes**, two big **telescopes**, and a **human skeleton model**. In the music room, there is a **grand piano**, an **upright piano**, many **recorders**, and other **musical instruments**. In the audio-visual room, there is a big **screen** on the front wall, a **projector** fixed to the ceiling, a **desktop computer** on the teacher's desk and many **laptop** and **tablet computers** for students. In the library, there are at least 20 thousand books, including **magazines**, **dictionaries**, and **audio-books**.

The **school year** starts in April and ends in March. We have **summer**, **winter**, and **spring holidays**, and these divide the year into **three terms**; the first, second, and third terms. At the end of each term, we write **report cards** on which all **grades** and **attendances** are recorded as well as teachers' comments. We have **annual events**, such as the **opening ceremony**, **school festival**, **sports day**, **school excursion**, and **graduation ceremony**. These school events are explained by homeroom teachers during the weekly **morning assembly** and the **homeroom gathering**.

Categories	Words/Expressions
Facilities	
Equipment	
Stationery	
Teaching Aids and Tools	
School Events	

(Some words could be included under more than one category.)

Chapter 1
Forming a Good Relationship with Students

I Vocabulary Preview   Match each word in Column A with a word or phrase in Column B of similar meaning. One has been done for you as an example.

Column A		Column B
1. adolescence (**d**)		a. foster, help grow up
2. enthusiastic ( )		b. belief in yourself and your abilities
3. obtain ( )		c. having or showing great interest
4. nurture ( )		d. teens, puberty
5. self-confidence ( )		e. get by effort

II Keynote Reading   The article below includes essential tips for you to put into practice in class. Read the article and answer the following questions.

    Teachers have the important responsibility of nurturing the development of young people from childhood **through to** adolescence. It is not surprising therefore, that teachers soon notice that students all have their own unique personalities. Some may be very outgoing and talkative; some can be troublesome, while others are quiet or even shy. Knowing how to establish good relationships with all types of students is a skill which teachers in training need to obtain.

    Many students, especially those who are enthusiastic or gifted, often impress the teacher by actively **participating in** classroom activities or expressing their personal opinions. The quieter students, however, are usually willing to remain silent and as a result, the others receive all or most of the teacher's attention. This imbalance can be corrected by making sure that quieter students receive more of the teacher's attention, for instance, **by way of** morning greetings and general conversation before and after class. This will **lead to** an increase in self-confidence in quiet students and potentially better results in class.

    The subject of English, more than other school subjects, enables the teacher to establish a close relationship with students through daily conversation, since it is **a means of** communication and not just a subject of memorization of grammar rules and vocabulary. This regular conversation will increase self-confidence in students and lead to a closer relationship between students and teachers.

Chapter *1* *Forming a Good Relationship with Students*

III Important Phrases/Words in the Keynote Reading

Fill in the blanks of the following sentences with the phrases/words in bold type in the reading passage.

1. _____ the beauty pageant is the first step to becoming a Hollywood star.

2. We are going to Beijing, the capital city of China, _____ Tokyo.

3. This northbound train goes _____ Union Station via Central Station.

4. The streetcar system was developed as _____ improving the traffic situation.

5. Your daily efforts will surely _____ great success in the future.

IV Listening Activity

Listen to the recording and fill in the blank spaces. Then learn the expressions for your future use.

(HRT=Homeroom Teacher, ALT=Assistant Language Teacher, SS=Students)

HRT: I'm your 1._____, Keiko Watanabe. Nice to meet you, class.

SS: Nice to meet you, Ms. Watanabe.

HRT: You 2._____ Keiko-sensei.

SS: Nice to meet you, Keiko-sensei.

ALT: I'm your 3._____, David Smith. Nice to meet you, class.

SS: Nice to meet you, Mr. Smith.

ALT: Call me David, everyone.

SS: Nice to meet you, David.

HRT: From today, David and I will teach you English.

ALT: I will help you 4._____ and 5._____ in English. Do you like English?

SS: Yes, we do.

HRT: That sounds great. 6._____ some games?

ALT: Let's play "Simon Says." Do you know the rules, class?

SS: Yes, we do.

ALT: All right. Stand up, everyone. Simon says, "7._____ three times." Simon says, "8._____." Put your hands down.

HRT: Oh, no one put their hands down. 9._____!

11

V Further Study

Give possible expressions of praise or encouragement similar to the two examples given below.

Good job, Kaoru!	Congratulations, Class!

VI Keeping a Class Journal

Listen to the recording and fill in the blanks.

It was my first day today to 1._____, Class 5B. I was 2._____ because I have never had 3._____ before. However, I 4._____ because all students were 5._____. Maybe it was because the students 6._____ and observed me 7._____ I was a good teacher or not. From today, 8._____ since I became an elementary school teacher two years ago, I have to 9._____ _____ all students and know them well to 10._____ _____ with each of them.

Chapter 1 Forming a Good Relationship with Students

Questions

Write your own journal answering the following questions. Suppose you were an elementary school teacher.

1. Which class did you meet for the first time in April?

2. Have you had the 5th graders before?

3. How did you feel on that day?

4. How do you describe your new students?

5. Why did you think students were also nervous?

6. When did you become a teacher?

7. What do you plan to do from today?

8. Why do you have to know your new students well?

....
....
....
....
....
....
....
....

VII Discussion Topics Discuss the topics below with your peers.

1. What should you do to form a good relationship with students?
2. How can that good relationship be maintained?
3. How can the student's confidence be won and maintained?
4. What should be done if a student appears to be emotionally upset?

Chapter 2
Cooperation with Assistant Language Teachers

I Vocabulary Preview Match each word in Column A with a word or phrase in Column B of similar meaning. One has been done for you as an example.

Column A		Column B
1. encourage ( )		a. smoothly spoken
2. hesitant (e)		b. think much of, regard highly
3. fluent ( )		c. spur on, give hope
4. fortunate ( )		d. lucky, successful
5. respect ( )		e. lacking decisiveness

II Keynote Reading The article below includes essential tips for you to put into practice in class. Read the article and answer the following questions.

In Japanese schools, Japanese teachers of English often **feel the need for** assistance from a native speaking English teacher when teaching the spoken language. These foreign teachers usually come from English speaking countries and **are known as** Assistant Language Teachers or ALTs, because they assist Homeroom Teachers, or HRTs in many team-teaching situations. It is important that HRTs and ALTs respect and **cooperate with** one another, especially when the HRTs do not have experience in speaking the language.

Differing opinions about teaching methods can sometimes arise, because of the difference in cultural background and the variation in teaching methods in other countries. Students who have both an HRT and an ALT are very fortunate because they can be made aware of cultural differences which are **closely linked to** the study of any language. In our globalized world, Japanese schools need an increasing number of ALTs from foreign countries, so that students can learn firsthand about life in other countries.

Although many HRTs may be a little hesitant to speak to ALTs in English **for fear of** making mistakes in front of their students, they should be encouraged to make the effort. When students see that their HRT is communicating with their ALT in English, they will realize the importance of being able to speak. Students will realize that they should try hard to speak English in order to become as fluent as their HRT.

Chapter 2 Cooperation with Assistant Language Teachers

III Important Phrases/Words in the Keynote Reading

Fill in the blanks of the following sentences with the phrases/words in bold type in the reading passage.

1. He couldn't come into the classroom _____ being scolded by the severe teacher.
2. The English language is _____ German and French.
3. Kyoto and Hiroshima _____ the most popular tourist spots in Japan.
4. Japanese always _____ help from resource-rich countries.
5. We will _____ the publishing company in developing the new teaching methodology.

IV Listening Activity

Listen to the recording and fill in the blank spaces. Then learn the expressions for your future use.

HRT: How was yesterday? Did you enjoy the classes?

ALT: Yes, I did, very much. What's happening today?

HRT: 1._____ has changed. We have three classes today, the second, third, and fifth periods.

ALT: All right. I'm 2._____ teaching Class 6A.

HRT: That will be in the second period, but why are you looking forward to it?

ALT: Because students said they are 3._____ about animals in English.

HRT: That's right. This is the curriculum for the 6th year. This month, we're going to teach about animals. Do you 4._____?

ALT: Let's see ... What can we do?

HRT: Can you talk about animals found in your country?

ALT: There are a lot in America, as you know. I'll 5._____ _____ using animal names.

HRT: Do you know any songs about animals?

ALT: *Old MacDonald Had a Farm* is the best one. They will love it and learn a lot about animals. That'll be very exciting.

HRT: Class will 6._____. Today, we will have class in the music room.

ALT: Let's see how it goes.

15

V Further Study

When working together with an ALT in class, what would you say to him/her in the cases below?

1. When the ALT is speaking too fast.

2. When the ALT is speaking too softly.

3. When students want to know a word in English.

4. When students want to know the spelling of a word.

5. When students want to know the pronunciation of a word.

6. When the ALT is using a word students do not know.

7. When students want to learn about other types of "furniture" in English.

8. When students do not know the difference in pronunciation.

9. When students want to know the difference in intonation.

10. When a student needs the ALT's help.

VI Keeping a Class Journal

Listen to the recording and fill in the blanks.

A new ALT came to our school 1._____ today. He 2._____ Class 5B. His name is David Smith and he 3._____ Nampa, a small city in Idaho, the USA. David told us about 4._____ Japan and the USA. He said that Japan is a small country and 5._____, while the USA is very big. He added that the USA is a multi-cultural country while Japan is often regarded as 6._____. He likes Japanese people because we are always 7._____. Everyone in Class 5B was very 8._____ and happy because David said Japan is his second home country.

Chapter 2 Cooperation with Assistant Language Teachers

Questions

Write your own journal answering the following questions. Suppose you were an elementary school teacher.

1. When did your ALT start at your school?

2. What is the name of the ALT and where is he/she from?

3. What does the ALT think about the differences between Japan and his/her country?

4. Why does the ALT like Japan?

5. Do your homeroom students like the ALT?

....
....
....
....
....
....
....
....
....
....
....

VII Discussion Topics Discuss the topics below with your peers.

1. What is the most important responsibility of HRTs in an English class?
2. What is the most important responsibility of ALTs in an English class?
3. In what ways can HRTs help ALTs before and after class?
4. In what ways can ALTs help HRTs before and after class?

Chapter 3

Groupism

I Vocabulary Preview — Match each word in Column A with a word or phrase in Column B of similar meaning. One has been done for you as an example.

Column A		Column B
1. isolate	(**d**)	a. not often
2. seldom	( )	b. manner of acting
3. impolite	( )	c. rude or not polite
4. behavior	( )	d. set apart from others
5. annoy	( )	e. disturb

II Keynote Reading — The article below includes essential tips for you to put into practice in class. Read the article and answer the following questions.

    Suppose an ALT asks Haruka to answer a question in class. Haruka does not answer but starts to ask the same question of her friend Yuriko sitting beside her. The teacher is shocked because he wants Haruka to answer the question and not Yuriko. Haruka successfully gets the right answer from Yuriko and gives it to the teacher. He **wonders why** Haruka did not give her answer directly to him. Is it because she did not know the answer and needed her friend's assistance?

    He just wanted to know Haruka's level of understanding but the answer he got came from Yuriko. The teacher wanted the student just to say "I don't know" directly to him if she did not know the answer. This kind of behavior by Japanese students often annoys ALTs.

    Haruka does not mean to insult the ALT, but she was just **not sure whether** her answer was correct and wanted her friend's support. This is only one example of Japanese "groupism." Japanese students often behave together as a group and seldom act individually. They do not want to be independent and even **are afraid of** being **isolated from** their group. ALTs who are new to Japan often experience this seemingly impolite attitude and feel ignored by Japanese students. To avoid misunderstandings between the ALT and students, the HRT can teach students to behave independently, to **look into** the ALT's eyes when they answer questions and to realize that knowing other manners and customs is part of language learning.

Chapter 3 Groupism

III Important Phrases/Words in the Keynote Reading

Fill in the blanks of the following sentences with the phrases/words in bold type in the reading passage.

1. Many students _____ making mistakes when speaking English.
2. The ALT often _____ most Japanese students are shy.
3. I am _____ the new homeroom teacher speaks English well.
4. Takeshi got feverish and was immediately _____ the rest of the students.
5. Emiko tried to _____ the teachers' room to see if her homeroom teacher was there.

IV Listening Activity

Listen to the recording and fill in the blank spaces. Then learn the expressions for your future use.

11

HRT: How do you like Class 5B students?

ALT: 1._____, I like them because they are friendly.

HRT: Yes, they are, David, but 2._____ by "generally speaking"?

ALT: Well, I'm often confused by some students' behavior.

HRT: How do they confuse you?

ALT: When I asked Yuri a question yesterday, she looked at Noriko and started talking. I 3._____ because she ignored me.

HRT: She didn't ignore you. She just didn't know the answer and asked Noriko for help.

ALT: Then, why didn't Yuri say, "I don't know" directly to me?

HRT: In Japan, 4._____ to ask your friend for help if you don't know the answer.

ALT: I don't think that's 5._____, unless they're working in groups.

HRT: All right, David, I'll tell them to give you their 6._____.

ALT: Thank you very much, Keiko-sensei.

HRT: Some students are very shy, but I'm sure they'll 7._____ _____.

ALT: I really hope so.

V Further Study

Learn the expressions of warning in the box below, and fill in the blanks with an appropriate expression to complete the sentences. There may be more than one possible answer.

1. When some students are noisy, the teacher might say, "_____"
2. When a student's behavior is not appropriate, the teacher might say, "_____"
3. When students do not pay attention to the teacher, she might say, "_____"
4. When a student disturbs his classmates, the teacher might say, "_____"
5. When the teacher cannot hear a student, he might say, "_____"
6. When students are running around in the classroom, the teacher might say, "_____"
7. When a student makes a mistake and others laugh, the teacher might say, "_____ He is trying hard."
8. When a student did not bring a textbook, the teacher might say, "_____"
9. When a student's exam results are not satisfactory, the teacher might say, "_____"
10. When a teacher asks the class to remember to submit their homework the following day, the teacher might say, "_____"

a. Be quiet, please.	b. Behave yourself, please.	c. I want you to do better in the future.
d. Speak up, please.	e. Please sit down.	f. Say it again in a loud voice, please.
g. Please stop talking.	h. Don't laugh, class.	i. Stop running around, please.
j. Be sure to bring your homework tomorrow.		k. Listen up, please.
l. Make sure you bring your textbook tomorrow.		m. Please pay attention to me, class.
n. Please don't forget your textbook tomorrow.		o. Speak clearly, please.
p. Make an effort to do better, please.		q. Don't disturb your classmates, please.
r. Please don't forget your homework tomorrow.		

VI Keeping a Class Journal

Listen to the recording and fill in the blanks.

After talking to David this afternoon, I realized that there is 1._____ _____ in characteristics between Japanese students and American students. David said that Japanese students are too 2._____ and tend to make groups. He also said that students should be 3._____ and express their own opinions. American students are trained to 4._____ _____ their early childhood. For example, parents usually give their children a bedroom to themselves even to 5._____ and they do not sleep with their children. I was shocked to hear that.

Questions

Write your own journal answering the following questions. Suppose you were an elementary school teacher.

1. Do you often talk to the ALT about your class?

2. What did the ALT say about the difference between Japanese students and American students?

3. What does the ALT think about the characteristics of Japanese students?

4. What does the ALT think about the characteristics of American students?

5. Were you shocked to hear the difference between Japanese students and American students?

....
....
....
....
....
....
....
....
....

VII Discussion Topics Discuss the topics below with your peers.

1. Do you like team sports or individual sports?
2. Were you a member of any clubs when you were in primary school?
3. Which do you feel more comfortable with, belonging to a group or being alone?
4. Do you think Japan is a group-oriented society?
5. If you do, how would you describe Japanese groupism?

Chapter 4
Inter-lingual Interference

I Vocabulary Preview Match each word in Column A with a word or phrase in Column B of similar meaning. One has been done for you as an example.

Column A		Column B
1. plural ( )		a. disturbance, something in the way
2. interference (**a**)		b. uncertain
3. ambiguous ( )		c. to stress, to underline
4. emphasize ( )		d. to watch attentively
5. observe ( )		e. more than one

II Keynote Reading The article below includes essential tips for you to put into practice in class. Read the article and answer the following questions.   13

    Japanese is an ambiguous language because the grammatical subject of a sentence is not usually mentioned, **except when** it should be clarified or emphasized. When you speak Japanese, you put the verb after the object, while the object comes after the verb in English. No plural forms are used in Japanese while in English there are many nouns which have plural forms or need an "s" **at the end** to make them plural. There are other structural differences between the two languages. 5

    Japanese students often make a sentence like "banana don't like" when they want to say "I don't like bananas." This is because they first **think of** the sentence in Japanese, where there is no subject and the object comes before the verb, and then translate it into English. During this translation process, the hidden subject should come first in an English sentence, and then the verb and the object. Moreover, "banana" should be in the plural form "bananas" even though no plural form is necessary in Japanese. 10

    When learning a foreign language, students **tend to** be influenced or affected by their mother tongue and apply its structure in their target language, which causes mistakes when they speak. This phenomenon is called inter-lingual interference and **observed quite commonly** in the language learning process. The ideal way to avoid this problem is to learn a foreign language while trying to avoid thinking in the mother tongue. 15

20

III Important Phrases/Words in the Keynote Reading

Fill in the blanks of the following sentences with the phrases/words in bold type in the reading passage.

1. _____ of the day, they decided the topic of their assignment.

2. Steve never pays attention to the teacher _____ the topic is about the new technology.

3. Teachers _____ pay attention to those students who do not participate in activities.

4. Can you _____ any good ideas for tomorrow's English lesson?

5. The new teaching system is _____ in private primary schools.

IV Listening Activity

Listen to the recording and fill in the blank spaces. Then learn the expressions for your future use.

HRT: You don't look happy. Have you got troubles?

ALT: I don't understand why Japanese students 1._____.

HRT: What kind of mistakes do you mean?

ALT: They usually don't 2._____, so I don't understand who they mean.

HRT: For example?

ALT: When they say, "sashimi like," does that mean, "I like sashimi" or "He likes sashimi"?

HRT: Now, I know what the problem is.

ALT: Why do they 3._____?

HRT: It's because when we speak Japanese, we 4._____.

ALT: I see. What do you think is the best solution?

HRT: That's very difficult to answer.

ALT: I guess, thinking in English might be the answer.

HRT: I agree.

ALT: They should 5._____ when they speak English.

HRT: I also have to try to think in English when speaking English.

V Further Study   Answer the following questions in a clear manner.

1. You don't like bananas, do you?

2. You know the way to the nearest station, don't you?

3. Aren't you American?

4. Don't you think you are good at English?

5. Your sweater was expensive, wasn't it?

VI Keeping a Class Journal   Listen to the recording and fill in the blanks.

David sometimes says that he does not understand my English. He does not complain about my pronunciation, but about 1._____.
For example, I said "no" when I should have said "yes" to his question, which was, "You've prepared for tomorrow's lesson, haven't you?" I often 2._____ _____ because I always think of an answer to his question first in Japanese and then 3._____. David's suggestion is that thinking in English is 4._____ the kind of mistakes which are caused by the differences between Japanese and English.

Questions

Write your own journal answering the following questions. Suppose you were an elementary school teacher.

1. Does your ALT understand your English?

2. What does your ALT say about your English?

3. How does your ALT specifically criticize your English?

4. What does your ALT tell you about the English spoken by Japanese?

5. What is your ALT's suggestion to avoid making mistakes?

....
....
....
....
....
....
....
....
....
....

VII Discussion Topics
Discuss the topics below with your peers.

1. When is the subject of a sentence unnecessary in English?
2. Do you give a direct "Yes" or "No" when answering a question in English?
3. Why do Japanese people tend to drop the articles when speaking English?
4. Why do Japanese people tend to drop the plural "s" when speaking English?
5. What happens if the positions of the subject and the object are changed in the following sentence — "The dog bit the girl"?

Chapter 5
British English and American English

I Vocabulary Preview — Match each word in Column A with a word or phrase in Column B of similar meaning. One has been done for you as an example.

Column A		Column B
1. vocabulary ( )		a. for this or that reason
2. horizon (e)		b. less, smaller
3. therefore ( )		c. forming words with letters
4. minor ( )		d. knowledge of words
5. spelling ( )		e. the junction of the earth and sky

II Keynote Reading — The article below includes essential tips for you to put into practice in class. Read the article and answer the following questions.

16

English language teachers often **wonder whether** they should teach British English or American English. British English is of course spoken in Great Britain, while American English is spoken in the USA. It is true that there are differences between the two, but when Britons and Americans speak to one another, they understand each other **without any difficulty**. This means that the differences between the two forms of English are only very minor. 5

English is spoken as the first language **not only** in Britain, the USA and Canada, **but also** in Australia, and New Zealand. It is also used as the official language in India, Pakistan, Singapore, and the Philippines, and as the second language in many other countries. **It is often said** that in some of these countries they speak British English, while in others they speak American English. It is not necessary, however, to differentiate between the two, because it cannot be said that one form of English is "more correct" than the other. Therefore, it would be nonsense to ask which is the best and which should be taught at school. 15

It is important, however, to know the differences between them, which are mainly in spelling, vocabulary and pronunciation, because this knowledge will broaden students' international horizons. They may have chances **in the future** to visit some countries where English is spoken as the first language, or where English is the common language, and enjoy learning the differences. 20

Chapter 5 British English and American English

III Important Phrases/Words in the Keynote Reading

Fill in the blanks of the following sentences with the phrases/words in bold type in the reading passage.

1. Sarina and her friends always _____ Hana speaks good English.

2. Hana speaks English _____ because she went to school in London.

3. Eri speaks _____ English _____ French because she was born in Quebec, Canada.

4. In Japan, _____ that students should be quiet and listen to the teacher in class.

5. Many students from my class say that they want to go to college _____.

IV Listening Activity

Listen to the recording and fill in the blank spaces. Then learn the expressions for your future use.

(ALT: Kevin from Britain)

S: How do you come to school every day, Kevin?

ALT: I usually 1._____ to come to school.

S: Oh, do you? 2._____ ?

ALT: About 15 minutes.

S: Only 15 minutes. Wow, you must walk very fast.

ALT: Walk? I said I take the underground.

S: 3._____ taking the underground?

ALT: I mean I come here by underground railway.

S: Oh, by subway. I thought you 4._____ an underground path.

ALT: Sorry I have confused you. We Britons call the subway the "Underground."

S: I see. What does the subway mean in Britain?

ALT: It means an underground path in Britain.

S: It's very confusing.

ALT: There are many other differences between British English and American English.

S: That sounds very interesting. Which is better?

ALT: Nobody can say which one is 5._____ . Both are good English.

S: I see, Kevin.

ALT: OK, I'll teach some of the differences in my next class.

S: I'm 6._____ more of these differences.

27

V Further Study

Fill in the blanks to complete the comparison table in order to learn the differences between British English and American English. Two have been done for you as examples.

Spelling Differences		Vocabulary Differences	
British English	American English	British English	American English
odour	odor	underground	subway
favour		queue	
humour		torch	
pyjamas		rubbish	
apologise		telly	
centre		flat	
cheque		lift	
programme		rubber	
traveling		1st floor	

VI Keeping a Class Journal

Listen to the recording and fill in the blanks.

There are two ALTs helping us at our school. David 1._____ Idaho and speaks American English. Kevin is from London and speaks British English. Both of them are 2._____ and we do not see any difference between their 3._____, but they say there are many differences in spelling, 4._____ _____. Kevin from England says Japanese students are used to American English because they 5._____ in their everyday lives. They like listening to American music and watching American movies.

Chapter 5 British English and American English

Questions

Write your own journal answering the following questions. Suppose you were an elementary school teacher.

1. How many ALTs are helping Japanese teachers at your school?

2. Who is the most popular ALT?

3. Where are the ALTs from?

4. Do they speak British English or American English?

5. What kind of differences do you see between British English and American English?

6. Are your students used to British English or American English?

....
....
....
....
....
....
....

VII Discussion Topics Discuss the topics below with your peers.

1. Are you able to hear the difference between British English and American English?
2. Which spelling are you familiar with, British or American?
3. Which pronunciation are you familiar with, British English or American English?
4. Do you think Japan is more influenced by the USA than by the UK?
5. In which countries is British English mainly spoken?
6. In which countries is American English mainly spoken?

Chapter 6
Teaching Aids

I Vocabulary Preview — Match each word in Column A with a word or phrase in Column B of similar meaning. One has been done for you as an example.

Column A		Column B
1. generation (**b**)		a. a period of one hundred years
2. implement ( )		b. age group
3. dominate ( )		c. simple, basic or original
4. century ( )		d. control or rule
5. primitive ( )		e. tool or device

II Keynote Reading — The article below includes essential tips for you to put into practice in class. Read the article and answer the following questions.

    It was thousands of years ago that primitive teaching methods began, when members of the older generations passed on their knowledge to the younger generations. Because the elders could neither read nor write, this method of teaching was done orally without the help of any specific tools.

    As time went by, tablets of stone or slate were used together with small pieces of white rock to use as chalk for drawing and later writing characters. Over the centuries these primitive implements have been replaced by blackboards, textbooks, notebooks, pens and pencils. **Apart from** writing instruments, teachers then used **a range of** teaching tools such as flash cards, models, pictorial materials, globes and maps. These items are normally referred to as teaching aids.

    More recently, electronic equipment such as computers, DVD players, and projectors are increasingly being found in school classrooms and are becoming necessary teaching tools. The introduction of this new technology into the classroom provides the teacher with valuable new tools for teaching, however, it also provides a challenge for teachers to **keep up to date with** the rapidly changing technology.

    Some scientists say that the day will come when artificial intelligence (AI) will replace human teachers. **No matter how** advanced the technology may become, however, machines will never be able to completely replace teachers, **as long as** human beings dominate the world.

III Important Phrases/Words in the Keynote Reading

Fill in the blanks of the following sentences with the phrases/words in bold type in the reading passage.

1. _____ hard you may work, you will never overcome the problem.

2. _____ English, what language would you like to learn?

3. I will go back to college in order to _____ the scientific innovation.

4. They never stopped their struggles _____ the dictator controlled the country.

5. _____, the two families became friendly and lived happily ever after.

6. The new textbook covers _____ topics regarding sociolinguistics.

IV Listening Activity

Listen to the recording and fill in the blank spaces. Then learn the expressions for your future use.

HRT: I'd like to 1._____ tomorrow afternoon.

ALT: Why are you going to use them?

HRT: We're supposed to teach about English speaking countries, and I have made a PowerPoint slideshow.

ALT: What did you 2._____?

HRT: The names of the countries, their capital cities, flags and locations on the world map.

ALT: What 3._____?

HRT: Could you teach them how to pronounce the country names?

ALT: Yes, I will. When shall I 4._____?

HRT: It will take me about 15 minutes to complete the slideshow, then I'll give you 5._____.

ALT: All right. Shall I ask the students to 6._____ before our class starts?

HRT: Yes please. Thank you for your assistance.

V Further Study

Fill in the blanks with the most appropriate word from the box below to complete the sentences concerning the teaching aid.

1. Utilizing _____ teaching aids in English classes helps to make teaching more effective and entertaining.

2. When a _____ is being used, the screen should be of an appropriate size so that all students have a clear view.

3. The teaching aid should be neither too difficult nor too easy and _____ the learning level of the students.

4. The teaching aid should be well-designed to _____ students to become more interested in the subject.

5. The teacher should be _____ to handling the teaching tool so as not to waste time during the class.

> motivate, meet, projector, audio-visual, accustomed

VI Keeping a Class Journal

Listen to the recording and fill in the blanks. 21

I made a PowerPoint slideshow last week and 1._____ _____ for the first time this afternoon. Students helped me set up the projector and opened 2._____. The slideshow was successful because I included 3._____ _____ in each of the slides. The presentation 4._____ _____ about English speaking countries; the country names, capital cities, flags and locations on the world map. David, the ALT, taught students 5._____ of the country names.

> **Questions**
> Write your own journal answering the following questions. Suppose you were an elementary school teacher.

1. What kind of teaching aid did you make last week?

2. When did you present the teaching aid to students?

3. How did students help you before you started teaching with the aid?

4. How effective was your teaching aid?

5. What did you include in your teaching aid?

6. What did you teach using your teaching aid?

7. What did your ALT help you with?

....
....
....
....
....
....
....

VII Discussion Topics Discuss the topics below with your peers.

1. Name some teaching aids and tools which are available at your school.
2. What teaching aid or tool do you use most frequently when teaching English?
3. Which teaching aid or tool do you think is the most useful when teaching English?

Chapter 7
Using the Tablet Computer in Class

I Vocabulary Preview — Match each word in Column A with a word or phrase in Column B of similar meaning. One has been done for you as an example.

Column A		Column B
1. device	( )	a. place in position for use
2. PE	(c)	b. tool, machine, or equipment
3. immediately	( )	c. physical education
4. extend	( )	d. instantly
5. install	( )	e. stretch out

II Keynote Reading — The article below includes essential tips for you to put into practice in class. Read the article and answer the following questions.

 New electronic learning devices are increasingly being introduced into classroom activities. One of the most recent of these devices is the tablet computer. When connected to the school Wi-Fi network, the tablet computer acts as an electronic textbook, notebook, writing device and audio/video player. It provides the student with an amazing new learning experience, which extends beyond the classroom to the outside world, through the use of software and connection to the Internet.

 Various software programs or apps enable teachers and students to perform an increasing range of tasks on tablet computers or mobile devices. Teachers can demonstrate to students how to use their creativity by writing stories, creating blogs, composing music, making educational videos, conducting chat sessions with students in other countries or using AI to obtain information. The advantages of these electronic devices can be seen across all the traditional school subjects, **such as** music, art, math, science, language and P.E.

 Another advantage of using the tablet computer is that, **provided** all teaching materials **are installed in** it, students **do not have to** carry a big backpack full of heavy books and are able to do their homework at home and submit it immediately to the teacher electronically. Some more advanced schools are **making full use of** the tablet computer for their online learning during the summer vacation, through which students perform required tasks by participating in a video chat session on a website. After the vacation they attend classes to discuss what they have learnt online.

Chapter 7 Using the Tablet Computer in Class

III Important Phrases/Words in the Keynote Reading

Fill in the blanks of the following sentences with the phrases/words in bold type in the reading passage.

1. Teachers _____ worry too much about students' family affairs.

2. The question is easy _____ you have studied the chapter beforehand.

3. New air-conditioners _____ classrooms on the second floor.

4. The subjects _____ arithmetic and social science are popular among students.

5. Even primary school students now are _____ high-tech devices.

IV Listening Activity

Listen to the recording and fill in the blank spaces. Then learn the expressions for your future use.

ALT: We are going to use our tablet computers in this period. 1._____ _____, please.

S1: Yes, David.

ALT: Are you 2._____ network? If not, 3._____ to access the school network.

S2: All right, David.

ALT: Tap the Pages icon 4._____. You'll find last week's review, "The Animals Living in Australia." You can 5._____ _____ and find your favorite animal.

S1: I like koalas.

S2: I can see many kangaroos. They're cool.

ALT: You can 6._____ the pictures if you want to see the details of the animals.

S1: Wow. Koalas are hanging onto a eucalyptus tree.

ALT: 7._____ and you can find the pictures of platypuses. They are found only in Australia.

S2: Awesome. Have you actually seen those animals in Australia?

ALT: Yes, I have, but only in a zoo.

35

V Further Study

Fill in the blanks with the most appropriate phrases from the box below to complete the sentences in order to learn how to use a tablet computer in English.

1. Enter your Wi-Fi _____ to access the network to go online.
2. On the home screen, tap one of the _____ to open it.
3. You could tap the Safari or Google button to display the _____.
4. Tap the YouTube app icon and _____ you want to view.
5. You could chat with your foreign friend on Skype _____.
6. The battery icon tells you when the battery is full or _____.
7. Your tablet computer automatically goes _____ when inactive for five minutes.
8. Press the _____ to go back to the home screen.

> free of charge, application icons, find a video, into sleep mode,
> home button, Web browser, running low, network password

VI Keeping a Class Journal

Listen to the recording and fill in the blanks.

There is a free 1._____ for my class tomorrow, and I have downloaded it 2._____. The app is useful because it teaches students how to read and write 3._____ _____. I am sure students will be happy to learn the alphabet on the tablet computer. First, David will teach them 4._____ _____ and use the app in English, and then I will do the same thing in Japanese. Another thing I should do tomorrow on the tablet is 5._____ _____, because we update it 6._____. I should ask David for help because he knows a lot about computer technology.

Chapter 7 Using the Tablet Computer in Class

Questions

Write your own journal answering the following questions. Suppose you were an elementary school teacher.

1. Are there any apps which English teachers must have for class activities?

2. If there are, have you downloaded any onto your tablet computer already?

3. How is the app useful for your teaching?

4. What kind of reaction do you expect from students when using the app?

5. Who is going to explain how to download and to use it in English?

6. Do you have a school homepage, blog, or Facebook page?

7. If you do, who updates it and how often?

8. Who helps you when you have computer troubles?

....
....
....
....
....
....
....
....

VII Discussion Topics Discuss the topics below with your peers.

1. In what class can you use a tablet computer?
2. What is one of the disadvantages of using a tablet computer in class?
3. What kind of apps do you need when you teach basic English?
4. Do you think pay apps are worth buying?

Chapter 8
Utilizing the Internet as Teaching Resources

I. Vocabulary Preview

Match each word in Column A with a word or phrase in Column B of similar meaning. One has been done for you as an example.

Column A		Column B
1. treasure ( )		a. proper or fitting for someone or something
2. ignore ( )		b. refuse to notice or recognize
3. up-to-date ( )		c. a large amount of wealth or property
4. appropriate (**a**)		d. basic or essential
5. fundamental ( )		e. current or in fashion

II. Keynote Reading

The article below includes essential tips for you to put into practice in class. Read the article and answer the following questions.

    The Internet is considered as a treasure island of teaching resources because it contains up-to-date information in almost all fields from basic to advanced stages. No teacher can ignore the advantages of utilizing the Internet where more and more pedagogical information has been accumulating.
    In terms of English teaching, teachers can google **a variety of** theses regarding teaching methodologies and techniques, teaching materials from fundamental to advanced levels, pronunciation demonstration videos, story-telling videos, and chants and songs on YouTube. There are so many teaching resources that teachers should carefully select materials of the most appropriate level for students.
    Teachers should also be careful not to be too **dependent on** materials taken from the Internet simply because they are useful but should be used as additional materials. Textbooks guide mainstream teaching and the Internet resources should be used to support it. Achieving a balance in resources is often difficult because students can easily become more interested in materials from the Internet than a textbook.
    Another point for consideration when using materials from the Internet is copyright restrictions because most of them are protected by copyright law and their usage is limited to classroom usage only. Moreover, teachers should reference their work making it clear where the materials originally came from by listing credits of the Internet sites. **Regardless of** how difficult the use of materials from the Internet may be, teachers **cannot help but** use these materials because it is said that all teaching materials including textbooks will be on the Internet eventually.

Chapter 8 Utilizing the Internet as Teaching Resources

III Important Phrases/Words in the Keynote Reading

Fill in the blanks of the following sentences with the phrases/words in bold type in the reading passage.

1. All students were accepted _____ their age or nationality.
2. We _____ respect the teacher because of his self-sacrificing conduct.
3. _____ educational programs have been telecast throughout the country.
4. _____ technological innovation, the university is second to none.
5. Some teachers are too _____ assistant language teachers.

IV Listening Activity

Listen to the recording and fill in the blank spaces. Then learn the expressions for your future use.

ALT: Your homework was 1._____, Kei.

S: Thank you very much, David. I took a lot of information from the Internet.

ALT: In that case, you 2._____ where you got the information.

S: I am sorry, but I did not know that.

ALT: Please be more careful in the future.

S: Yes, David.

ALT: 3._____, because I should have told you about plagiarism.

S: What is it?

ALT: Plagiarism is 4._____. Illegal means 5._____, and we should list the sites of the original writing to avoid plagiarism.

S: I see. That's something my friends would not know. Thank you, David.

ALT: All right, Kei. (To himself) I also have to 6._____ _____ next time.

V Further Study

Fill in the blanks with the most appropriate words so as to complete the passage regarding how to use the Internet for language learning.

A 1._____ on the Net like Skype is very useful for 2._____. Students can find their 3._____ living in foreign countries and 4._____ in English. What they have to do is to 5._____ to the Internet and 6._____ the Net chatting program, and find chat-mates through a language 7._____. Students are also able to learn English by watching 8._____ on YouTube. Many of these videos are so 9._____ that students can learn English and the culture of English speaking countries. After finishing Net learning, students have to log off and 10._____ the computer.

> well-designed, language learning, exchange information,
> chat-mates, download, exchange site, chat system,
> shut down, log on, English lesson videos

VI Keeping a Class Journal

Listen to the recording and fill in the blanks.

When I need additional teaching materials, I often 1._____ _____. This is because I can easily find useful and 2._____ _____ on the Internet. There are photos, graphs and tables, graphics, and video clips. I often 3._____ _____ for children. Today, I showed "Hokey Pokey" to the class and they liked it very much. The video included not only the lyrics, but also 4._____ _____. David taught students how to sing and 5._____. Students were really having a good time, while I had a hard time practicing dancing because I am not a good dancer.

Questions

Write your own journal answering the following questions. Suppose you were an elementary school teacher.

1. How do you usually find additional teaching materials?

2. What kind of teaching materials can you find on the Internet?

3. What sort of teaching materials do you often use in class?

4. What type of additional teaching materials did you use today?

5. How did students like the additional teaching materials?

6. How did the ALT help you?

....
....
....
....
....
....
....
....
....
....

VII Discussion Topics Discuss the topics below with your peers.

1. What is your opinion of illegal copying?
2. What kind of examples would you give to explain illegal copying?
3. Why do people buy illegally copied products?

Chapter 9
Untranslatable Expressions

I Vocabulary Preview Match each word in Column A with a word or phrase in Column B of similar meaning. One has been done for you as an example.

Column A		Column B
1. counterpart (**e**)		a. a prayer said before eating
2. occasion ( )		b. something that is the same or equal
3. grace ( )		c. talk between people
4. conversation ( )		d. a time of something happening
5. equivalent ( )		e. a person or thing having the same function or characteristics as another

II Keynote Reading The article below includes essential tips for you to put into practice in class. Read the article and answer the following questions.

    Students often ask the teacher what the English expression is for "itadaki-masu" or "gochiso-sama," which Japanese people usually say **before and after** eating. Students think that there is the same custom in English speaking countries. The fact is, however, that people in many countries do not have such a custom **except when** some Christians may say grace before meals.

    Another example is that Japanese say "itte-kimasu" to their family when leaving home, and "tadaima" when coming back home, and "itte-rasshai" and "okaeri-nasai" **in reply to** these greetings. Students naturally think that there are English counterparts to these Japanese expressions and want to use equivalent English words at home and at school.

    There are no exact translations for these Japanese expressions because people in English speaking countries usually do not have any special common **set patterns** when eating or leaving home. Word-for-word translations, for example "right now" for "tadaima," would mean nothing in English on such occasions. Therefore, it is important for the teacher to explain the cultural differences to students and, **if necessary**, find possible equivalent expressions in English which could be used in similar situations.

    In English speaking countries, children may say "See you" to their parents when leaving home for school, and Dad and Mom may say "Have a good day" to their children. When parents **are invited to** a friend's dinner party, they may say "Oh, this looks tasty" before eating and "That was delicious" after finishing a particular dish. But practice with natural conversations and situations, and not set patterns, will help the students to use the correct expression in such daily situations.

Chapter 9 Untranslatable Expressions

III Important Phrases/Words in the Keynote Reading

Fill in the blanks of the following sentences with the phrases/words in bold type in the reading passage.

1. The problem has been solved, but _____ a reinvestigation will be done.

2. The greeting card reads, "You _____ my 12th birthday party."

3. These are the spoken _____ used by salespeople when selling second-hand cars.

4. _____ the question, he referred to an article in *The New York Times*.

5. You should take two aspirin tablets _____ each meal.

IV Listening Activity

Listen to the recording and fill in the blank spaces. Then learn the expressions for your future use.

29

HRT: Do you have any questions, class?

S: 1._____ "itadaki-masu" in English?

HRT: That's a difficult question. Shall we ask David?

S: Yes, let's.

HRT: David, we 2._____. How do you say "itadaki-masu" in English?

ALT: We don't say anything in English. You can start eating when a meal is served 3._____.

HRT: Isn't it 4._____?

ALT: Not at all, because that's our custom.

HRT: I see. Do you understand what David said?

S: Yes, I do. I won't say anything when eating from now on.

ALT: That's not 5._____, Sakura. In Japan, you should say "itadaki-masu" before you start eating.

S: Why?

ALT: That's your custom in Japan. Each country has its own tradition. 6._____ _____ is very important.

HRT: Absolutely. That's another important area of foreign language teaching.

43

V Further Study

Fill in the blanks with possible cultural English equivalents to the Japanese expressions given below. More than one correct answer is possible. Two have been done for you as examples.

Japanese	Said When	Possible Cultural English Equivalents
Itadaki-masu	Before eating	*Oh, this looks tasty. / Looks delicious.*
Gochiso-sama	After eating	*That was delicious. / It was good.*
Itte-kimasu	Leaving home	
Tadaima	Coming back home	
Otsukare-sama	Parting	
Ganbatte	Encouraging	
Yoroshiku	Meeting	

VI Keeping a Class Journal

Listen to the recording and fill in the blanks.

It was an interesting day because one of my students asked me how to say "itadaki-masu" in English. I was 1._____ the question so I asked David about the same question. His answer was 2._____ because he said 3._____ without saying anything in the USA. David added that 4._____ when he started eating without saying a word, meanwhile his host family 5._____ they had said "itadaki-masu" all together. I thought that everyone would say something like "I'll start eating," at meal time in English speaking countries. My idea was 6._____.

44

Chapter 9 Untranslatable Expressions

Questions

Write your own journal answering the following questions. Suppose you were an elementary school teacher.

1. What kind of day was it for you today?

2. What kind of English question did your students ask you?

3. Were you ready to answer the question?

4. Do you usually ask the ALT for help when you cannot answer the question?

5. What was the ALT's answer to that question?

6. Did the ALT tell you about any embarrassing experiences in Japan?

7. What did you think about the embarrassing experience?

....
....
....
....
....
....
....
....

VII Discussion Topics Discuss the topics below with your peers.

1. When would the Japanese expression "otsukare-sama-desu" be used?
2. What does this expression in Japanese mean to an English speaking person?
3. What is an equivalent expression that could be used which is similar in meaning to "tsumaranai-mono-desu"?
4. Some people say that this traditional way of speaking is fading away. Why is it?
5. Do you think this expression is still important in Japanese society?

Chapter 10
Slang and Informal English Expressions

I Vocabulary Preview Match each word in Column A with a word or phrase in Column B of similar meaning. One has been done for you as an example.

Column A		Column B
1. criticize	(**d**)	a. following social rules
2. scenario	( )	b. unpleasant, disgusting
3. offensive	( )	c. refined in manners
4. formal	( )	d. find fault with
5. polite	( )	e. outline of a play or drama

II Keynote Reading The article below includes essential tips for you to put into practice in class. Read the article and answer the following questions.

31

    Slang is a very informal, usually spoken language used especially by particular groups of people. It is usually not included in basic English textbooks and therefore not taught in class. What annoys teachers is, however, the fact that students are often **tempted to** use informal language, thinking it is, as they say, "cool" and **different from** others. They pick up such expressions as "See ya" meaning "I'll see you later" and "Check it out" meaning "Look at this." These expressions are quite commonly heard in English speaking countries and found in movie scenarios. What **is wrong with** learning and teaching these informal expressions?

    The problem is that students use them without knowing when and how to use them. In a sense, slang expressions are difficult to use because, even though polite native speakers may use them when speaking to their close friends, they would not use them to someone in a position **superior to** them, or when writing to them. If they did, they could be criticized by others for not being polite or educated. Therefore, it is difficult for non-native speakers to judge correctly the place, time, and occasion where they can use slang expressions.

    HRTs **as well as** ALTs should first teach formal and everyday English to beginner students because such English is accepted anywhere in the world, but slang and informal expressions may not be understood correctly. Teachers should also teach students never to use swear words or offensive "four-letter words" even if the students already know them.

Chapter 10 Slang and Informal English Expressions

III Important Phrases/Words in the Keynote Reading

Fill in the blanks of the following sentences with the phrases/words in bold type in the reading passage.

1. Jun's school is _____ Kei's in early childhood education.
2. What you said today is _____ what you told me yesterday.
3. Students _____ all teachers had to take part in the evacuation drill.
4. Something _____ the photocopier because it makes a strange sound.
5. Students were _____ swim in the river because the water was crystal-clear.

IV Listening Activity

Listen to the recording and fill in the blank spaces. Then learn the expressions for your future use.

ALT: All right, did you enjoy singing the new English song?
Ss: Yes, we did, David.
ALT: Before 1._____, I'll give you some homework.
S: Damn it!
ALT: What did you say, Kei?
S: I said, "Damn it!"
ALT: Who taught you the expression?
S: I learned it when 2._____.
ALT: Do you know the meaning?
S: No, I don't, but I heard it many times in shocking scenes.
ALT: You 3._____ again.
S: Why can't I?
ALT: It's 4._____ in class in Japan.
S: Is it such a bad expression?
ALT: Yes, it is. It's 5._____.
S: What's the meaning of "offensive"?
ALT: It could 6._____ or insulted.
S: I see. I'll never use it again.
ALT: OK, Kei.

V Further Study

Below are sentences including informal expressions that are now normally heard in everyday life. Fill in the blanks with their formal counterparts. Two have been done for you as examples.

Informal Expressions	Formal Expressions
Dad and Mom	*Father and Mother*
Grandpa and Grandma	
The teacher said, "You guys."	
The ticket costs 20 bucks.	
He looks so cool.	
I wanna go there.	
I gotta go.	*I have got to go.*
They're gonna be here soon.	
Bye for now.	
"That's awesome!" said Jackie.	

VI Keeping a Class Journal

Listen to the recording and fill in the blanks.

I was shocked today because one student used 1._____ _____ in class. The ALT caught the word and 2._____ _____ again. I know some students 3._____ _____ slang expressions because they think it fashionable to learn 4._____. I think, however, we cannot blame those students because there are a lot of 5._____ _____ which include offensive slang words and expressions. David said that it is almost impossible for us to 6._____ those expressions.

Questions

Write your own journal answering the following questions. Suppose you were an elementary school teacher.

1. How do you feel if a student uses offensive English slang expressions in class?

2. Do you think your ALT should scold students for using offensive slang expressions?

3. Why do you think some students are interested in using offensive slang expressions?

4. Do your students regularly watch many video games and violent movies?

5. Do you think these games and movies include offensive slang expressions?

6. Do you and your ALT think it possible to stop them from using offensive expressions?

....
....
....
....
....
....
....
....

VII Discussion Topics Discuss the topics below with your peers.

1. Do you use slang or informal expressions when talking in Japanese?
2. Why do you think using slang expressions is not advisable in your work life?
3. What are the demerits of using slang expressions?
4. What are the merits of using slang expressions?
5. Are there any English slang or informal expressions which you know?

Chapter 11
Practicing English with Other Activities

I Vocabulary Preview Match each word in Column A with a word or phrase in Column B of similar meaning. One has been done for you as an example.

Column A		Column B
1. realize ( )		a. the reason for the action
2. strengthen ( )		b. understand, be fully aware of
3. motivation (**a**)		c. spread out
4. immersion ( )		d. being deeply absorbed, completely covered
5. expand ( )		e. make strong or stronger

II Keynote Reading The article below includes essential tips for you to put into practice in class. Read the article and answer the following questions.

Elementary school students in Japan have only a few hours of English learning each week. They hardly have a chance to speak English outside of school hours, **unless** they attend a special private English tutorial school. Many students tend to lose interest in learning English when they have no chance to use it in a real life situation. They begin to think that English is only one of the subjects they must learn at school like math, science, and sociology. Students will only **become motivated** when they truly realize that English is a means of communication, and when they are able to make themselves understood in English.

In order to strengthen and maintain their motivation for learning English, HRTs should give students as many opportunities as possible to speak English, **apart from** regular English classes. The best way to do this is for HRTs to speak English **as much as possible**, even when doing other activities. English Immersion Education is such a program where all subjects and activities are given in English except when teaching Japanese. As students become used to hearing more English, HRTs can expand their usage of the language to other school activities throughout the entire day. It is certain that this strategy of HRTs, **in cooperation with** ALTs, will encourage students to speak English more often.

Chapter 11 Practicing English with Other Activities

III Important Phrases/Words in the Keynote Reading

Fill in the blanks of the following sentences with the phrases/words in bold type in the reading passage.

1. We study English _____ learn what is happening in the world.

2. You can practice English every day _____ your teachers and friends.

3. We will have Nature Study outside tomorrow _____ it is rainy.

4. Students are asked to study _____ before the "Vocab Contest."

5. We have the "Vocab Contest" every year so that students will _____ to study new words.

IV Listening Activity

Listen to the recording and fill in the blank spaces. Then learn the expressions for your future use.

HRT: What's the best way to learn English, David?

ALT: Speak English every day 1._____, Keiko-sensei.

HRT: But we have only a few hours of English every week.

ALT: Can students practice it with their friends and parents?

HRT: No, that's difficult. We need to give them more chances to speak English.

ALT: I'm always 2._____ in English during breaks.

HRT: That's only a few minutes.

ALT: OK, 3._____ any of your homeroom activities? We can sing English songs, and practice the "Radio Gymnastics" together in English.

HRT: That's wonderful. Everyone likes singing English songs. How can we practice "Radio Gymnastics" in English?

ALT: I can teach them many expressions doing that, for example, "4._____," "bend your knees," "5._____," and such and such.

HRT: You're such a wonderful teacher.

ALT: And also, they can visit me in the teachers' room after school if they want to talk to me in English.

HRT: I really 6._____.

51

V Further Study

What kind of basic English phrases would you need to use when doing other classroom activities such as singing and decorating the classroom?

Singing	Decorating the Classroom
Please listen to this song now.	Let's draw flags of some countries.

VI Keeping a Class Journal

Listen to the recording and fill in the blanks.

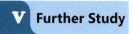

Most students want to speak more English at school, but the number of English classes is limited. I asked David 1._____, and his answer was that we should provide a better 2._____.
So, I asked him to try to translate the things in the classroom in English, and stick the names on each of them. Some students cannot read them but it is all right because the stickers 3._____ to be more interested in English. I also asked David 4._____
_____, friends and buildings from his hometown. Students now 5._____
_____ and asking David questions about the pictures.

Chapter 11 Practicing English with Other Activities

Questions

Write your own journal answering the following questions. Suppose you were an elementary school teacher.

1. Do you think students want to speak more English at school?

2. Do you think students need more English speaking activities?

3. Have you asked your ALT for his/her ideas to make the classroom more international?

4. What were your ALT's suggestions?

5. Have you asked your ALT to show some family pictures to class?

6. What is the reaction from students?

....
....
....
....
....
....
....
....

VII Discussion Topics Discuss the topics below with your peers.

1. How can you make an English speaking atmosphere in your homeroom?
2. Do you need a more English speaking atmosphere in your school?
3. How can you make your students speak more English at school?
4. What are other school activities where English is useful?
5. Have you ever tried to use English in those activities?

Chapter 12
Gestures—Non-verbal Communication

I Vocabulary Preview Match each word in Column A with a word or phrase in Column B of similar meaning. One has been done for you as an example.

Column A		Column B
1. verbal ( )		a. show, mean
2. indicate ( )		b. a situation where things are badly organized
3. facial ( )		c. a movement to communicate a feeling
4. gesture ( )		d. using spoken language
5. confusion (**b**)		e. on the face

II Keynote Reading The article below includes essential tips for you to put into practice in class. Read the article and answer the following questions.

    Understanding speakers' facial expressions and body language is very important when people speak **with one another**, especially when the communication **is taking place** between people of different cultures. Non-verbal communication including postures, facial expressions, eye contact, and gestures often **means more** than verbal or spoken communication. Native English speakers use more gestures than Japanese people, while Japanese **tend to** restrict facial expressions and body language.

    ALTs often use gestures when teaching English to students, which sometimes causes misunderstandings or confusion for students. Therefore, it is very important for students to know the meanings of common gestures made by native English speakers. The most popular of those gestures, for example, made by native English speakers is a shrug or raising of the shoulders, which is often seen in movies, and it indicates, "I don't know," or "There's nothing I can do about it." Many Japanese students know the meaning of this gesture and some of them use it jokingly when they do not know an answer in class, which **is disrespectful to** the teacher.

    Another example is "fingers crossed," which is a hand gesture used to **wish for good luck**. For instance, when an ALT introduces a new English game, crossing her index and middle fingers means that she hopes the game will be a success. There are many other gestures which ALTs use and students enjoy learning and using in English classes.

Chapter 12 Gestures—Non-verbal Communication

III Important Phrases/Words in the Keynote Reading

Fill in the blanks of the following sentences with the phrases/words in bold type in the reading passage.

1. Pointing _____ others not only in Japan, but in many other countries.

2. The Winter Festival _____ now in many kindergartens around Norway.

3. When teaching English, HRTs and ALTs should cooperate _____ all the time.

4. The day will come when love _____ to you than money.

5. People often _____ when seeing a shooting star.

IV Listening Activity

Listen to the recording and fill in the blank spaces. Then learn the expressions for your future use.

38

S: 1. _____?

ALT: Yes, certainly. What is it?

S: 2. _____ rubbing your finger and thumb together?

ALT: Where did you see that?

S: When I was watching an American movie.

ALT: Were the movie characters talking about money?

S: Yes, they were. 3. _____?

ALT: That gesture means counting dollar bills, or "money."

S: That's interesting. Do you also 4. _____ kissing the tips of your fingers? I saw it in the same movie.

ALT: It was a scene where someone was eating, right?

S: That's right. How did you know?

ALT: The hand gesture means "delicious." It's 5. _____.

S: After finishing the meal, the actor gestured like that to the waitress. Do you use these gestures yourself?

ALT: Me? No, I don't, because some gestures may seem impolite.

S: Are there 6. _____?

ALT: Yes, there are. Gestures are just like a spoken language. They 7. _____ and from place to place.

55

V Further Study

Match each expression/expressions below with a gesture in the box. One has been done for you as an example.

1. Come here, please. ( )
2. He is a so-called "doctor." ( )
3. You did a good job. ( )
4. Quiet, please. Listen up, please. Shhh! ( )
5. I wish you good luck. ( )
6. So so. Neither very good nor very bad. ( )
7. Please stop it. Wait. ( )
8. I can't hear you. Speak louder, please. ( )
9. That's all right. OK. ( )
10. Call me, please. (J)
11. Is it me? ( )
12. I don't know. There's nothing I can do about it. ( )

A	B	C	D	E	F
G	H	I	J	K	L

VI Keeping a Class Journal

Listen to the recording and fill in the blanks.

Leonard is an Italian-American ALT, and he uses gestures 1._____

_____. At first, students did not 2._____,

but they have gradually come to understand 3._____

_____ the gestures. For instance, he uses the "cheek screw," or pressing a

forefinger into the cheek and rotating it, meaning delicious, or lovely. He said that

gestures can 4._____. As a Japanese

5._____ using foreign gestures, but students enjoy

using some of the gestures which Leonard has taught.

Chapter 12 Gestures—Non-verbal Communication

Questions

Write your own journal answering the following questions. Suppose you were an elementary school teacher.

1. What country is your ALT from?

2. Does the ALT use gestures when teaching English?

3. Do students understand these gestures?

4. Describe one gesture that your ALT often uses in class.

5. What is the ALT's opinion about using gestures?

6. Do you feel comfortable or uncomfortable when you use foreign gestures?

7. Do your students enjoy learning and using foreign gestures?

....

....

....

....

....

....

....

....

VII Discussion Topics Discuss the topics below with your peers.

1. Do you think using gestures encourages students to learn a foreign language?
2. Have you used any Japanese gestures which ALTs do not understand?
3. Have you noticed any ALT's gesture that you do not understand?
4. Did you know some gestures have different meanings in different cultures?
5. What other foreign gesture do you know?

Chapter 13
Foreign Loan Words

I Vocabulary Preview Match each word in Column A with a word or phrase in Column B of similar meaning. One has been done for you as an example.

Column A		Column B
1. contribute ( )		a. the way a language is spoken
2. pronunciation ( )		b. minus, or unfavorable
3. trend ( )		c. give, add
4. negative ( )		d. badly behaved
5. naughty (**d**)		e. a general tendency

II Keynote Reading The article below includes essential tips for you to put into practice in class. Read the article and answer the following questions.

40

There are **a large number of** foreign loan words used in the Japanese language, most of which are written in *katakana* script. The Japanese people, **generally speaking**, often like to use loan words, as they believe these words make their conversation sound more fashionable or sophisticated. This belief leads to the misunderstanding among Japanese that such foreign words are English, when **in fact** they come from a variety of foreign languages. Words such as "*pīman*" and "*shūkurīmu*," from French, and "*arubaito*," from German, are typical examples. During English classes, students may often say "I don't like *pīman*," **instead of**, "I don't like green peppers."

In addition, the Japanese pronunciation of English loan words has a negative effect on the student's ability to pronounce the same word correctly in English. The loan word "*sutajio*" is pronounced as "studio" in English and "*stajiam*" is actually "stadium" when pronounced correctly in English.

To make matters worse, many of these loan words do not have the same meaning in Japanese as they do in the original language. Typical examples of these are the English words "steering wheel" of a car, known in Japanese as "*handoru*", originally handle, and the personal characteristic of being "cunning" in English has changed its meaning in Japanese, where the word "*kan'ningu*" means to cheat. Modern trends in language have also contributed to these differences in meaning. The loan word "*yankī*" or Yankee now means a naughty child and not just a citizen of the US.

Chapter *13* Foreign Loan Words

III Important Phrases/Words in the Keynote Reading

Fill in the blanks of the following sentences with the phrases/words in bold type in the reading passage.

1. _____, his house caught fire after being damaged by the earthquake.

2. _____ coming himself, the president sent his secretary.

3. _____, owning a smartphone is becoming a necessity.

4. _____ Chinese tourists have visited Japan in recent years.

5. Spanish and Italian are alike. _____, they are in the same language family.

IV Listening Activity

Listen to the recording and fill in the blank spaces. Then learn the expressions for your future use.

ALT: Today, 1._____ you know already. Do you know any English words, Toru?

S1: I know many; "*kirin*," "*monkī*," "*terebi*," "*gēmu*," …

ALT: 2._____, Yuri?

S2: Yes, I know some; "*pīman*," "*naihu*," "*rajio*," and …

ALT: Good, boys and girls. Is "*kirin*" an English word?

S1: I think so, because it is written in *katakana*.

ALT: *Katakana* words 3._____.

S2: I know, "*kirin*" is "giraffe" in English.

ALT: That's right. 4._____ is called a giraffe. How about "*monkī*"?

S1: "*Monkī*" is an English word!

ALT: Yes, it is, but it is "monkey," not "*monkī*." How about "*pīman*"? Do you know what it is?

S2: My father said it's an English word.

ALT: I'm sorry, but it's not. It's "green pepper" in English. Don't you think it's fun to learn new words? 5._____; "monkey," "giraffe," and "green pepper."

V Further Study
Rewrite the underlined words below into correct English.

1. I have *arubaito* from 3:00 this afternoon. _____
2. Please fill in this *ankēto* form. _____
3. Let's play *toranpu* together after school. _____
4. Mary keeps her old books in a *danbōru* box. _____
5. We used a *gasukonro* to cook rice. _____

VI Keeping a Class Journal
Listen to the recording and fill in the blanks.

During my 1._____ this morning, some students 2._____ _____ about foreign loan words. They thought that all *katakana* words were 3._____ and they were 4._____ _____ in conversations. I told them that *katakana* words 5._____ _____ English, and gave them homework 6._____ of 20 *katakana* words. In my next English class, I will teach them which *katakana* words are originally from English, and the 7._____ of the words.

Chapter 13 Foreign Loan Words

Questions

Write your own journal answering the following questions. Suppose you were an elementary school teacher.

1. What were your students confused about this morning?

2. Did your students think that all foreign loan words are English?

3. When did your students think they were able to use *katakana* words?

4. What did you tell them about *katakana* words?

5. What did you give them to do as homework?

6. What will you teach your students about *katakana* words?

7. What else will you teach your students?

....
....
....
....
....
....
....
....

VII Discussion Topics Discuss the topics below with your peers.

1. How many foreign loan words do you think you use in your daily life?
2. Name some loan words originally from the English language.
3. Do you think foreign loan words are helpful or confusing when teaching English?

61

Chapter 14
ESL vs. EFL

I Vocabulary Preview Match each word in Column A with a word or phrase in Column B of similar meaning. One has been done for you as an example.

Column A		Column B
1. dominant (**e**)		a. shortage, absence
2. mall ( )		b. identify, understand, acknowledge
3. lack ( )		c. a walkway with shops on each side
4. recognize ( )		d. successful, useful, active
5. effective ( )		e. having primary control or influence

II Keynote Reading The article below includes essential tips for you to put into practice in class. Read the article and answer the following questions.

 Suppose you were a Japanese student staying in London to study English. You would be studying English at a language school where all teachers are of course Londoners and students are from around the world. After school, you would go back home and talk to your host family in English, practicing new vocabulary and expressions you have just learned at school. At a nearby shopping mall, you would do your shopping using English. This would be an ideal English learning situation and **is regarded as** learning English as a second language, or ESL, because this language of English is your second language enabling you to **get along** in London.

 On the other hand, studying English in Japan where Japanese is the dominant language is regarded as EFL or English as a foreign language. In an EFL situation, English classes are the only places where English is used, and students rarely have a chance to speak English outside of school. Therefore, students have to **concentrate on** studying English at school while teachers have to give students as many opportunities as possible to speak English **to compensate for** the lack of contact with the language every day.

 Both HRTs and ALTs should recognize the differences between ESL and EFL **making the most of** teaching materials and devices, and always trying to find the most effective way to teach the language.

Chapter 14 ESL vs. EFL

III Important Phrases/Words in the Keynote Reading

Fill in the blanks of the following sentences with the phrases/words in bold type in the reading passage.

1. Japan _____ a mono-cultural society, but actually it isn't.
2. This teaching system is designed for _____ the Internet.
3. We can't _____ studying in summer because it is too hot.
4. I hope to _____ by myself when I am on holidays in Japan.
5. The boss allowed his secretary an extra day-off _____ having worked overtime.

IV Listening Activity

Listen to the recording and fill in the blank spaces. Then learn the expressions for your future use.

44

HRT: What did you do before coming to Japan?

ALT: I actually taught English in London to ESL students from all over the world.

HRT: Oh, did you? What are 1._____ teaching in Japan and Britain?

ALT: There are many differences.

HRT: For example?

ALT: When I was teaching in Britain, students were 2._____ _____ so English was the only common language in class. That's why it was time consuming to teach 3._____ _____ only in English.

HRT: On the other hand, I think all students we teach in Japan can understand Japanese, so it's easy to explain new words and expressions in Japanese.

ALT: That's right. Another difference is that students studying in Britain are surrounded by English 4._____ _____. They can use what they've learned right after school.

HRT: They are ideal surroundings to learn a language.

ALT: In Japan, English classes are the only chance for most students to practice English, so time is important. They 5._____ _____ the practice time and speak English as much as possible in class.

HRT: I agree, and so we should teach 6._____ _____ vocabulary and expressions.

ALT: Our teaching materials are made to fulfill those EFL teaching aims in Japan.

HRT: I see that teaching English in Japan is not an easy task.

ALT: No, it's not.

63

V Further Study

Choose a word from the box below which describes each of the various types. One has been done for you as an example.

	Various Types
flower	tulip, rose, dandelion, hydrangea, chrysanthemum, etc.
	sardine, tuna, bonito, shark, carp, saury, eel, etc.
	lion, elephant, giraffe, alligator, jaguar, gorilla, etc.
	museum, hospital, church, station, condo, skyscraper, etc.
	spinach, cabbage, celery, onion, lettuce, carrot, radish, etc.
	gold, silver, copper, iron, steel, aluminum, tin, lead, etc.
	jacket, pants, sweater, coat, shirt, skirt, shorts, parka, etc.
	chair, sofa, bench, stool, saddle, throne, etc.
	dragonfly, butterfly, ladybird, beetle, grasshopper, cicada, etc.

insect, building, fish, animal, vegetable, metal, clothes, seat, flower

VI Keeping a Class Journal Listen to the recording and fill in the blanks. 45

I asked David what 1._____ was for teaching English. His answer was that he tries 2._____ in class. He said the teacher's job is to encourage students to 3._____

_____ in class, because most students in Japan have no time to speak English outside of school. Another tip David gave me was that the teacher should choose the most basic and useful vocabulary, 4._____

_____ even difficult things in easy English.

Chapter 14 ESL vs. EFL

Questions

Write your own journal answering the following questions. Suppose you were an elementary school teacher.

1. What is your ALT's first suggested tip for teaching English in Japan?

2. What is the reason for the first suggestion?

3. What is your ALT's second suggested tip for teaching English in Japan?

4. What is the reason for the second suggestion?

5. Do you think you can use those tips yourself?

....
....
....
....
....
....
....
....
....
....
....

VII Discussion Topics   Discuss the topics below with your peers.

1. Where did you learn English?
2. What is the difference between learning English abroad and in Japan?
3. Do you think the ALT should use only English in class?
4. Do you think the ALT should use Japanese when teaching English?

Chapter 15
An Additional Reason for Studying English

I Vocabulary Preview Match each word in Column A with a word or phrase in Column B of similar meaning. One has been done for you as an example.

Column A		Column B
1. souvenir	( )	a. reason, aim, goal
2. discriminate	(c)	b. memento, token, reminder
3. abroad	( )	c. separate, differentiate
4. purpose	( )	d. bring up, raise
5. foster	( )	e. to or in a foreign country

II Keynote Reading The article below includes essential tips for you to put into practice in class. Read the article and answer the following questions.

One of the most important purposes of English education is to foster the love of the English language among Japanese school children. When Japanese businesspeople go abroad, their English ability helps them almost anywhere in the world since English is the most spoken and the most studied language worldwide.

There are **huge numbers of** tourists visiting Japan every day and Japanese people working in airports, hotels and souvenir shops need English to assist those visitors. When foreigners want to stay in Japan **for a long period of time**, however, they will notice that Japanese is the dominant language and will start studying Japanese. Then, is studying English a waste of time if students do not go abroad or work at an airport or a hotel? **On the contrary**, studying English has another very important purpose.

Even if students have no chance to speak English abroad or at their workplace in Japan in the future, in their English classes they should learn foreign cultures and ways of thinking to broaden their outlook of the world. Fostering international minded Japanese is another very important factor of English education, which will help Japanese citizens to understand foreigners, even when they speak with each other in Japanese. **In this way**, Japanese people will realize that their own culture is not necessarily better or more important than others. Students should learn that there are people of different skin colors, cultures, languages, and religions in this world, and should learn to avoid discriminating against others **on the basis of** these factors.

Chapter 15 An Additional Reason for Studying English

III Important Phrases/Words in the Keynote Reading
Fill in the blanks of the following sentences with the phrases/words in bold type in the reading passage.

1. Teachers are usually employed _____ their academic and career records.

2. You will make the same mistake again and again if things continue _____.

3. Reading and writing were stressed in English education _____ _____.

4. _____ papers and books regarding education have been published.

5. I first thought she was diligent, but _____ she was lazy.

IV Listening Activity
Listen to the recording and fill in the blank spaces. Then learn the expressions for your future use. 47

S: My father said he studied English a lot at school but he can't speak it.

ALT: 1._____. Many Japanese people say the same thing.

S: I don't think English is necessary in Japan. I have never spoken to anyone in English in Japan.

ALT: 2._____ a foreign country?

S: No, never.

ALT: English is useful 3._____ or work at an airport.

S: I've got no plans to travel. Then, why do I have to study English?

ALT: That's a good question.

HRT: We teach you English because we want you to be good English speakers.

ALT: And 4._____.

S: What's that?

HRT: English is spoken and studied in most countries around the world, so you can learn and understand about them in our English classes.

S: 5._____ there are many pictures of different countries on the walls?

HRT: That's right. We should know about 6._____.

ALT: Your father doesn't speak English, but he surely knows about the world.

S: Yes, he does. Now I understand what you mean. Thank you very much.

67

V Further Study

In each of the following sentences, select the correct words from the alternatives given in the brackets, in order to learn more about the English language and the English speaking world.

1. There are more than (a. 7.5 billion b. 75 billion) people living in the world today.

2. Following Chinese, English is the (a. second most b. third most) spoken language worldwide.

3. About (a. 3.5 million b. 350 million) people speak English as their first language.

4. When combining native and non-native speakers, there are approximately (a. 18 billion b. 1.8 billion) English speakers in the world.

5. It is estimated that approximately (a. 80 percent b. 8 percent) of English speakers are non-native speakers.

6. In some countries English is an official language because of the influence of (a. American culture b. British colonization).

7. There are some (a. major dialects b. major varieties) of English, such as American English, British English, Indian English, Canadian English, Australian English, and New Zealand English.

8. English is considered as a "lingua franca" or a common language between speakers whose (a. second languages b. native languages) are different.

VI Keeping a Class Journal   Listen to the recording and fill in the blanks.

David told me that English is the most spoken and 1._____ _____ in the world. 2._____ actually speaks English and many more study English in Europe, Central and South America, Africa, Asia, and the Middle East. Therefore, English is very 3._____ _____ in those countries, and also to know about 4._____. We should tell students the fact that studying English will surely help them 5._____ _____.

Chapter 15 An Additional Reason for Studying English

Questions

Write your own journal answering the following questions. Suppose you were an elementary school teacher.

1. Have you talked with your ALT about the English language?

2. What did the ALT say about the reason why English is taught in Japan?

3. Do you know how many people speak English in the world?

4. Do you know in which countries English is spoken and studied?

5. Give two major reasons why learning English is so important.

6. Do you think that learning English will help students in their future?

....
....
....
....
....
....
....
....
....
....

VII Discussion Topics Discuss the topics below with your peers.

1. Name 6 countries where the official language is English.
2. Have you talked in English with people from any of these countries?
3. Have you talked in English with people whose native language is not English?
4. What kind of English differences have you noticed between native speakers and non-native speakers?

Chapter 16
Assessing English Ability

I Vocabulary Preview Match each word in Column A with a word or phrase in Column B of similar meaning. One has been done for you as an example.

Column A		Column B
1. evaluate ( )		a. basic, fundamental
2. foundational ( )		b. obtain, get, receive
3. integrate (d)		c. meeting face to face
4. acquire ( )		d. make into a whole, become one
5. interview ( )		e. grade, rate or assign a rank

II Keynote Reading The article below includes essential tips for you to put into practice in class. Read the article and answer the following questions.

It is not a simple task to evaluate a student's language ability, which **consists of** such skills as listening, speaking, reading, and writing. Therefore, when a teacher evaluates a student's language ability, these foundational skills are first **taken into consideration**. However, they do not stand alone, but are integrated when communicating with others.

In the early stages of language education, oral communication skills should be taught first, **in the same manner as** young children acquire their mother tongue. In more advanced stages, students learn to integrate their oral skills with written communication skills. Student evaluation, however, should not be based only on test scores, but also on participation in class activities, enthusiasm and attitude towards learning.

Teachers also should observe students' progress in English **based on** their students' reflection on the lessons. In the reflection period, students comment on the English lessons they had and on what interested them. **At the same time**, the reflection helps students understand the purposes of the lessons and hopefully encourages them in their study of English. Teachers themselves can also assess their lessons and find problems students could be facing.

There are several ways to actually assess beginning-level students' language ability, such as recitation, speech, role-play, show-and-tell, story-telling, and interview. Students are asked to perform a presentation **in front of** the class, either individually or in groups. Some performances may include language and cultural knowledge which they have **become aware of** during the lessons or from what they have acquired through their personal experiences.

Chapter 16 *Assessing English Ability*

III Important Phrases/Words in the Keynote Reading

Fill in the blanks of the following sentences with the phrases/words in bold type in the reading passage.

1. She has practiced the piano _____ Frederic Chopin did.
2. The teacher gave an A grade to Emiko _____ her exam results.
3. The research group _____ five young and energetic mathematicians.
4. Japanese teachers have now _____ the importance of public speaking.
5. Pronunciation should be _____ when language ability is assessed.

IV Listening Activity

Listen to the recording and fill in the blank spaces. Then learn the expressions for your future use. 50

HRT: What do you think of Class 5B so far, David?

ALT: Generally speaking, they are getting much better than 1._____ _____.

HRT: I think some are still less confident than others in speaking in English.

ALT: Yes, they should be made aware of 2._____ to improve their English.

HRT: How do you measure their English ability?

ALT: That's so difficult, Keiko-sensei, because we should 3._____ of their English.

HRT: For example, pronunciation, intonation, vocabulary and …

ALT: Yes, but these are only a few elements of students' English ability. We should also 4._____ to communicate with each other in English.

HRT: What do you think is the most effective way to measure their English?

ALT: There's no perfect way, but an interview might be 5._____ _____.

HRT: Why do you think so, David?

ALT: Well, because, showing 6._____, we can check their integrated English ability including their cultural knowledge, pronunciation, and even their attitude when expressing themselves in English.

HRT: I think I should explain to the students in Japanese 7._____ _____ the interview test for next week.

ALT: Thanks, Keiko-sensei. I'll prepare an interview picture card to ask them about their birthdays and birthday presents.

HRT: Sounds great. That will be exciting.

(See the sample Interview and reflection sheets on pages 74-76.)

V Further Study

Choose a word from the box below which is described in the definition column. One has been done for you as an example.

> Assessment, Dictation test, Placement test, Achievement test,
> Final test, Cloze test, Quiz, Multiple-choice test, Mock test

Vocabulary	Definition
Assessment	a test taken by a student so that teachers can judge their level or progress
	a short informal test
	a test in which a piece of writing is read to students learning a language, to test their ability to hear and write the language correctly
	a test consisting of a piece of text with words missing that students have to fill in
	a test taken at school for practice before a real test
	a test in which students are given a list of answers and they have to choose the correct one
	a test that measures a student's ability in order to place that student in the correct class or group
	a test that is designed to determine what students have learned over a particular period
	a test taken at the end of a school year or term

VI Keeping a Class Journal

Listen to the recording and fill in the blanks. 51

We had 1._____ today. David said it is a common classroom activity in English speaking countries. Students brought their family photos from home, showed them and 2._____ _____ to the class. We helped students prepare for their presentations 3._____ _____. Therefore, most students were 4._____ _____ in front of the class, but some were nervous and not successful in their presentations. Show-and-tell is effective to help students 5._____ public speaking. It is also a good opportunity for teachers to assess the students' English ability and 6._____ _____.

Chapter 16 Assessing English Ability

Questions

Write your own journal answering the following questions. Suppose you were an elementary school teacher.

1. When did you have a show-and-tell presentation in your class?

2. What did the ALT say about show-and-tell?

3. What did students bring from home?

4. What did students show and explain about to the class?

5. How did you help students for their presentations?

6. Were students confident or nervous in speaking in front of the class?

7. How is show-and-tell effective?

....
....
....
....
....
....
....
....
....

VII Discussion Topics Discuss the topics below with your peers.

1. Why do you think assessment is necessary?
2. What methods are there to assess a student's oral English ability?
3. What methods are there to assess a student's written English ability?
4. How do you utilize the assessment results?
5. What do you have to pay attention to when giving any kind of assessment?

73

Interview Test

"When is your birthday?"

The interview is designed to test the student's ability to perform the following; (1) correctly pronounce the months indicated by the teacher, (2) combine correctly the numbers and the months to give a particular date, (3) give the date of the student's birthday, and (4) talk about what the student wants for his/her birthday.

Interview Procedure: The HRT/ALT asks students to come to the front of the classroom one by one. Showing the Interview sheet to the student, the teacher begins the interview by asking questions. Some sample questions and answers are as follows. (See the Interview sheet on page 75.)

Teacher	Student
Hi, Sakura. This is your interview card.	Thank you, Keiko-sensei.
Please read these three months aloud. (Pointing to any three months.)	March, July, and November.
Please read any month and any number to give a date.	Yes, March 4, July 15, and November 21
In what month were you born?	I was born in June.
When is your birthday exactly?	My birthday is June 23.
Do you know any of your friends' birthdays?	Yes, I do. I know Hiro's birthday.
When is his birthday?	It's October 27.
Now please take a look at these pictures, Sakura.	Yes, Keiko-sensei.
What are these? (Pointing to three items.)	It's a watch. It's a book. It's a soccer ball.
What do you want for your birthday?	I want a dress.
Good job. Thank you Sakura. That's the end of the interview test.	Thank you.

Reflection

After the interview test, the HRT explains in Japanese how to fill in the Reflection sheet. Students may fill in the sheet either in Japanese or English. (See the Reflection sheet on page 76.)

Interview: When is your birthday?

1 2 3 4 5 6 7 8 9 10 11 12
13 14 15 16 17 18 19 20 22 23
24 25 26 27 28 29 30 31

My Reflection

Unit Title: **When is your birthday?**

Name: _____ Date: _____

How did you like Unit 2?

1. Choose the face which shows how you feel.

   Very Good   Good   OK   So so   Not Good

2. Write three things/items you have learned in this unit.

1
2
3

3. Is there anything you did not understand?

4. Write your comments about the lesson.

   Note: Explanation required in Japanese.

QUICK REFERENCE FOR CLASSROOM ENGLISH

Below is a collection of common classroom expressions, which would be useful for teachers in charge of early stage English education classes. The following expressions are classified according to classroom activities from beginning to end of an elementary English lesson.

1. **Before starting a lesson**
   Hi, everyone.
   Good morning, class.
   Good afternoon, everyone.
   Stop talking, class.
   We won't start until everyone is quiet.

2. **Calling the roll**
   I'll call the roll.
   Is Junko here?
   Where is Tomoko?
   Who is absent today?
   Who isn't here today?
   Is Ichiro absent today?

3. **Checking students' health**
   How are you, everyone?
   How do you feel this morning?
   What's wrong with Emi today?
   Why were you absent yesterday?
   What's the matter with Hiroshi?

4. **Reprimanding late comers**
   Did you oversleep?
   Leave home ten minutes earlier.
   Don't be late tomorrow morning.
   Don't let it happen again.

5. **Starting a lesson**
   Everybody, please pay attention.
   Let's begin our English lesson.
   Are you ready for your English lesson?
   We'll learn how to write the ABC today.
   Open your textbooks to page 15.

6. **Giving activity instructions**
   Look at activity 3 on page 15.
   You need pencils.
   You need scissors.
   You have 15 minutes to do the activity.
   Put everything away.
   Turn to page 16.
   Put your desks together.
   Listen to the recording, please.
   Who would like to read?
   Do you want to answer question 3?
   Make pairs.
   Change partners.
   Get into groups of four.
   Make four teams.
   Sit in a circle.
   Mark the right answer.
   Could you try the next one?
   Move your desks to the back.
   Put your textbooks away.
   Make two lines.
   Clap your hands three times.
   Let's count from one to ten.
   Color the car red.
   Circle the right answer.
   Fold it in half.
   Cut out the picture.
   Glue it onto your notebook.
   Please repeat after me.
   Everybody, please stand up.
   Put your hands on your heads.
   Touch your toes.
   Once again, please.
   Put your pencils down.
   Come to the front of the class.

7. **Making sure students understand**
   Are you with me?
   Do you follow me?
   Do you understand?
   Can you see what I mean, Sakura?

8. **Checking the answers**
   Let's check the answers.
   Do you want to answer the question?
   Show me your answers, please.
   Come out and write it on the board.
   Write your answers on the whiteboard.
   Try to answer the question once again.

9. **Giving feedback to students**
   Very good.
   That's very good.
   Well done.
   That's nice.
   You did a great job.
   Fantastic!
   That's correct.
   That's quite right.
   You've got it.
   You've improved a lot.

10. **Encouraging students**
    Have a go.
    That's interesting!
    Never mind.
    Don't worry about it.
    That's a lot better.
    You were almost right.
    You've almost got it.
    There's no hurry.
    We have plenty of time.
    Have a try.
    It's OK to make mistakes.

11. **Giving homework**
    There is no homework today.
    Don't forget your homework, please.
    Take a worksheet when you leave.
    This is your homework for today.
    Prepare the next chapter for Monday.
    Do exercise 6 for your homework.

12. **Ending a lesson**
    That's all for today.
    It's almost time to finish.
    We have to stop here.
    I'm afraid it's time to finish now.
    Did you enjoy today's class?

13. **Getting ready to leave school**
    Put your books away.
    Pack your things away.
    Pack up your textbooks and pencils.
    You can go now.
    Goodbye, everyone.
    Have a nice weekend.
    See you tomorrow morning.
    Have a good holiday.
    See you again next Monday.

14. **Having special occasions**
    Enjoy your summer vacation.
    Merry Christmas and a Happy New Year!
    I hope you all have a good Christmas.
    Happy New Year, everyone!
    Happy Easter.
    Have a nice flight back, David.

Classroom Language for Students

I'm sorry I am late.
I don't understand.
Is this OK?
Please repeat that.
One more time, please.
I need your help, Keiko-sensei.
Can I talk to you for a minute?
Can I go to the washroom?
Can I come to the teachers' room now?
When is the homework due?
I couldn't answer the homework.
How do you spell the word?
Could you please give us an example?
How do you pronounce this word?
What's the difference between "A" and "B"?

Methods and Techniques of Teaching Basic English
—for the Teachers of Tomorrow—
児童英語教育のための方法と技術

Copyright © 2019
by
Masayuki Aoki / Peter Williams (ed.)

All Rights Reserved.
No part of this book may be reproduced in any form without written permission from the author and Nan'un-do Co., Ltd.

Illustrations by Yasco Sudaka
(p.3, 12, 24, 44, 60)

著作権法上、無断複写・複製は禁じられています。

Methods and Techniques of Teaching Basic English [B-892]
—for the Teachers of Tomorrow—
児童英語教育のための方法と技術

1　刷　2019年4月1日

著　者　青木雅幸　　　　　　　　　　Masayuki Aoki
　　　　ピーター・ウィリアムズ（監修）　Peter Williams (ed.)

発行者　南雲　一範　Kazunori Nagumo
発行所　株式会社　南雲堂
　　　　〒162-0801　東京都新宿区山吹町361
　　　　NAN'UN-DO Co., Ltd.
　　　　361 Yamabuki-cho, Shinjuku-ku, Tokyo 162-0801, Japan
　　　　振替口座：00160-0-46863
　　　　TEL：　03-3268-2311（営業部：学校関係）
　　　　　　　03-3268-2384（営業部：書店関係）
　　　　　　　03-3268-2387（編集部）
　　　　FAX：　03-3269-2486
編集者　伊藤　宏実

組　版　柴崎　利恵

装　丁　NONdesign

検　印　省　略

コード　ISBN978-4-523-17892-7　C0082

Printed in Japan

E-mail：nanundo@post.email.ne.jp
URL：http://www.nanun-do.co.jp/